AN ALICE AND A BOB

The names Alice and Bob are commonly used placeholders for archetypal characters in fields such as cryptography and physics. The names are used for convenience, since explanations such as "Person A wants to send a message to person B" can become difficult to follow, especially in complex systems involving many steps.

AN ALICE AND A BOB

SECTIONS CHAPBOOK SERIES
No. 2

By

Travvis Largent

USPOCO BOOKS
Phoenix, AZ

USPOCO BOOKS, a non-profit publisher, is a division of **us poetry company**.

All rights reserved under International and Pan-American Copyright Conventions. Published in the United States by USPOCO BOOKS, Phoenix, AZ.

uspocobooks@gmail.com

ISBN 978-0983306283
Library of Congress Control Number:

FIRST EDITION

CONTENTS

The Nature of Theory

Alice observes a couple in the park, their gestures.

Hypothesis: they are lovers on a picnic:
he traces her jaw line, thumbs her chin;

Hypothesis: he is blind and she his instructor:
behind sunglasses, he constructs her image,

mapping the border of her cheek; Hypothesis:
he is a friend easing the grief of a loss;

he wipes away the tear that mars her face.
All that remains is the proving: filling the gaps

in the theory and predicting the future.

Cepheid Variants

Bob in a box, a cubicle gently
described as an office with its
one strong lamp turned toward
a screen to illuminate the negatives
of the universe. In his pictures,
space is a creamy soup with stars
like flies littering the surface. He wants
the ones that consistently flicker,
the stuttering light that reveals
distance, which means time.

Here is maybe the age of the everything
spread on a desk. Make of the data
what it should say, like linking stars
into constellations, dots becoming strings
of the story of beginning to end.
Let the form arise from the data.

Theory hates and loves gaps.
You project what should fill
the space, imagine the missing
link. Here he finds only gaps:
that grad student hasn't returned
with coffee; his phone hasn't rung;

frames are missing: from five
to seven, a mote shivers, a shift
in the missing sixth frame; between
is an answer, or a clue, a hand
stroking a remote face for a reason.

Barycenter I

Alice calls from Oklahoma City,   and Bob

is in Arkansas.   Somewhere in

between   their voices meet, a common point

in the land of red earth,   somewhere they

can speak out of turn, the conversation

rolling from mouth to   ear, a tiny kissing

tongue that dissipates   into photons.

He calls from Arkansas,   and she is in Texas.

It is common, then, for   the choked conversations

that meet in the   clear-cut wastes of the Ouachita

National Forest,   the toppled trees silent

as the rumor of   fallen leaves in wind, to meet

their own hush,   the silence of too much

distance, of an uncertainty of space and their place.

To My Information Age Thisbe

each electron along this string
of phone lines courses
just to you

fires first in my skull
snakes on dendrites
clenches muscles
the diaphragm contracts
my lips and larynx shove air
tongue dances across breath
tints it with sound
turns thought kinetic
to tremble the thin receiver
that makes these words electricity
so they may sprint through
the cables across Texarkana
and Texas to set a ringing
in your home
to let your handset translate
again into moving air
these words vibrating your ear
made electricity again in you

unpacking boxes
I found
cradled in a pillowcase
one gold curl

Arguing Goldbarth

Alice wraps herself in a cream sea of cotton,
those parts that are blanket and the parts
that are Alice cuddling in electromagnetic
force, the same force that keeps that ring
on the nightstand from inhabiting the spaces
in her finger that aren't finger, or keeps Bob
from truly entering her the rare times they both try.
It's the tension that yields sensation,
not tension of skin on skin on ring on blanket
but of mutual force fields crackling as each
pushes against the other. So perhaps the idea
is that the wrapping matters: the hand grasping
the blanket's edge, the legs' tangled geometry,
the strong want against the weak nuclear force.

From Alice in California to Bob in Connecticut

Strange to find these trees, the Methuselah,
the bristlecone pines strangling stones
for some nourishment, famous for seeing
the twentieth century twice. They're always
almost dying, year after century after millennia.

Remember the story of the researcher
who read of Methuselah and so cut
one bristlecone down and cried at the five
thousandth ring he counted that night?

The severity of living alone makes them eternal,
the drought and wind, and a metabolism
for striving in this moonscape. We
cannot do this. The Q of my cigarette
in my ashtray doesn't stand for quality
of life or quantity, but a quick march to endings.

It isn't the struggle that makes our lives longer;
it's the nourishment we receive from sources abundant:
the sun, the fields, your stealthy hand
throwing my packs away. Meet me soon.
We're not like these trees.

Equivalences: (d=rt) = (d/r=t) = (d/t=r)

Don't slow down. Distance is divided
by your speed, a bar of broken
asphalt sung by engine and wheel.
Move, my love, like an excited
atom. A highway mile is a token
forty-eight seconds when you speed.

Distance over time, how we rate
our progress, my sweet, the components
from sharing keys to our first time,
the now and Lebanon's first date:
our momentum and moments,
movement, distance over time.

There is no overtime, my dear,
nothing to break this tie,
no golden goal fired at fine pace,
covering distance, a fine try.
Accelerating slows time; relativity's queer.
Come, my love, cover uncovered space.

Alice with Voyeurs

You go through door after door:
what a potent symbol it is
we watch you in silks framed
by the bedroom door.

The bathroom door you open and close.
modesty keeps us from looking in
the privacy not of private parts
but of your private functions

Out the front door by eight
to make the office door by nine.
your boss' lips are a trapdoor
he wants you to fall through

You press your hands to your face
after your manager leaves *your fingers*
a door shut against sight
go back through the kitchen door

by six to open the refrigerator door,
the smallest room in the house
that you only peek into. *don't go in*
you'd freeze – it's where you keep

all the other perishables Then back
to the bedroom door, unless this is
one of those times for long baths
that seep into your skin, wrinkling fingers.

Does it help you sleep? Does it wash

away the work of the day? Nothing for it;
it's just a symbol Now, at last,
we've been waiting for you to come

on to the bedroom door, which stays closed
until the time, late in the night, when you
finally lie down, shrug off the day, *watch*
yourself reenact it all in a dream, and sleep.

Octave: Nemesis Star

You'll be coming soon to the stones,
somewhere there, in the dark
beneath these trees, your little brown
body floating, a warm, dim star
naked in this evening, moving
closer to mine through the heady
night, where I'm trembling
in the moonlight, alive and ready.

.

Alice Explains Supernovae

we talk about beginnings   birth
in the paisley shape   of gases
welling from stars

the expended fuel   hydrogen used up
imploding   to explode
and waving out   like curled hair
memories of lovers   kinklets
in the universe

everything out of this
we are made   of stars
recombined elements thanks to fusion
hydrogen transmuted into odder
elements   my carbon and calcium
and protein shifted   from burning star
into the wavy curls   that you have
left   over on your pillows

Heilegenschein Aubade

Dew blankets the skin the sleeping bag
doesn't cover. Morning's rich light
wakes last night's invisibles: your leg
across mine, the thin hairs at the height
of your hip, a lust of strawberries
about your lips and mine, tiny traces
lingering as evidence of shared
kisses in other, unbared places.

It is early; I must go.
Our wildlife weekend is bookended
by a job I'd rather quit. I lean over
to kiss that hip; the light bends
around my shadow – above my other
shape, a halo on your skin hovers.

Alice & Bob at Home

Something nothing like sex
for her, it is a Sunday afternoon chore,
vacuuming the odd aggregate of skin
and dust and mites and ash. She drives

the vacuum, back and forth, sawing
at the shag, raising the fat yarns
of the carpet with suction to create
a strange chiaroscuro of overlapping

lines where the fibers catch light differently.
Out and back, in and out, she pushes
from her body, hand tight on the ribbed
handle, the fat head of the cleaner

roving over the same square inches
of carpet, the hairs rising and falling,
flattened under the shrill whine
of the engine like a semi's wheels

trundling by. The reeling fan inside
whips the whirlpool of air to make an
emptiness, the vacuum of the name,
a void that impels a filling, the rush of things

unwanted into the dark center of the vacuum
bag, filled now with the detritus of living
in their space. Here is the weekly chore,
the acts that mar an otherwise interesting

matrimony. While he does dishes in the other

room, another cleansing unlike sex, she is finishing
by herself, turning off the machine, reaching
into the vacuum to remove the bag and all

it pulled inside. The room now clean,
no one would dare to come inside, to sully
the renewed carpet, while he racks
the last of the dishes in the other room.

Trojans

It's just one more thing between us,
Bob says, but he's got ulterior motives.
It's a thin protection against things we
don't really need to be protected from:
our love, our promises, the honest
diving in to what we're supposed
to commit. He only wants a sensation,
the skin on skin, the way bodies slurp
at each other. He wants to inhabit
me completely; they want that:
a way to pass the thin door
between them and me
that keeps them, them,
and me, my own.

"c"

Alice has vomited every morning
for a week. They don't talk
about it. They've been trying
too long, months of waiting
for a week without sterile
napkins and blood. Vomit
is a good sign, is a cause
for hope. They won't taint
this by speaking – it may be
that there's an inert ball
curled inside her. It could
be his cooking. Still, both count
themselves to sleep in names:
Charlie, Charlene, Chris or Cara.

Cargo Cult Love

Alice rises first and begins breakfast
as Bob shambles out the door
for the paper. He makes her coffee
then packs his lunch while she showers.
They trade warm goodbyes at the carport.

He drives to work. So does she.
She generates reports and maximizes
productivity between cigarette-
and coffee-breaks. He designs
product rollout platforms after a vodka
tonic lunch. They take a meeting
together at Whole Foods at six and
arrange their appetites into a feasible
menu. A helpful clerk mediates
conflict over the wine selection.

He is tasked with vegetable preparation
and chops dutifully. She stuffs the chicken.
They talk briefly over wine about their days.
He watches Sportscenter while she
surfs the web for vacations far away.
He showers at night; she falls asleep
to meditation CDs. They lie unconscious
and experience REM sleep. Late-night
flights thrum distantly overhead.

Barycenter III

The event came; a particle spun
in each direction. They faced an issue
of who was first: Alice flung

an accusation and determined his
response. A redness, first at his crown,
something like an electric hiss,

started at the back of his head, crept
around his scalp, a wave parting
to become at his lips a tsunami-crest.

And so it was a charged particle
came between them, her
observation, his in parallel,

and these related to a field that slithered
through time: As it was and will be
and ever: The tiniest thing will gather

and grow into a well of gravity, a deep
pock in the space-time of the universe
of two; they will navigate the weave

of space that changes constantly, parsing
arguments as Pioneer missions
to a territory vaguely known, charting

the new meteor, the fresh region
of asteroids that signals the collision
of rocky planets, the flowering sun

or fading star, all the potential
pitfalls, the deep wells of gravity
they'll be in danger of crashing into.

Libration

Alice will rock in her sleep
like this, all night, her back
mostly to me, the night

light shadowing her shoulder
with a glow that widens
with each turn, but not enough

to show her face or feelings,
or give me anything but
her back. Tomorrow,

she will forgive whatever
was said, and forget. We
will embrace over coffee

and partings at the carport.
And at night, the silhouette
of her back will wave to me.

Noetic

You have a mind of mathematics,
always figuring the sum of the square
of some strange triangulation that tells
how far we are from Lebanon,
Kansas, from that first meeting. We're not
in Kansas anymore. The straw I'm stuffed
with is itching; I could while away
the hours, picking tiny flowers,
and counting he-loves-me's.

I could want to do some thinking
about us, about the phone calls
that always seem to pass through
Lebanon, but it's all a war of words,
of your thinking and my scratching
at the hollow shafts that poke
through my shirts. It's not that
there's nothing in here. I've an animal mind
that won't define distance the way you do.
There's only here and not. Mr. Wizard,
it's not that hard a concept.

Schrödinger's Cat

Bob is gone to a conference, again, which is no
different than each of the other times he has gone,
though he's taken that young assistant, which is
no different than any of the other times, except
that she is attractive and young, but married
some fresh seven months, and all Bob talks about
anyway is his presentation on superpositions, the dirty
jokes he tells about porn stars and Batman, jokes she
is too flighty to get, a lecture she is too dis- to organize.

They're sitting in a box of a hotel room,
working in the late of night, him correcting
the slide show, touching the curve of her young,
attractive knee, leaning close to read the monitor,
their cheeks almost touching–
                                                    She's sitting opposite
him, resolutely trying to take notes on the laptop,
thinking about her make-up and sheer dress,
sullen about missing the nerds' mixer downstairs
while he yammers about things invisible.

Half of married men are unfaithful in some way;
half of married women as well. And they are sitting,
alone, in this box, waiting for me to make an observation,
to open the door I have claimed a key to, to prove
my hypothesis, to skin a dead cat or a live one.

Retarded Ball

[F]or an ordinary "retarded" ball, Alice, in the emission, recoils opposite in space to the direction that the ball is moving. Bob, in the absorption, recoils in the same direction that the ball had been moving to cause a mutual repulsion between Alice and Bob. In contrast, for the "advanced" magic ball time traveling to the past, the situation reverses. – Dr. Jack Sarfatti

Alice and Bob stand on roller skates
on a frozen lake, ice as far as the eye
can travel. She holds a bright red ball
a foot from Bob and hurls it hard as she can.
It doesn't even reach escape velocity,
much less c. They drift apart.
He fires a return pass, hoping, a touch
of english on the ball. The distance blossoms
between them. The ice remains unfazed.

If this were dream, or some other dimension,
they could exceed the physics, break through
those Einsteinian limits, the ball magically
shifting from her to him pre-instantly,
the emission drawing them closer together. But here
reality intrudes. They are at opposite horizons,
now, almost disappearing behind
the curvature of the Earth. She yells to the mote
of a man, *What happened to the magic?*

Sestet: Death Star

Come, crater my body with lipstick,
with the impact of droplets of sweat,
build the shockwave with your fingers,
give me the firestorm of your nails,
drop matches on my skin – leave me
some scar before your orbit pulls you back.

Alice in Cozumel

Lights like pearls
on a string of electricity
run the edge of the pier,

the last halogen sign
a single light blinking
its red warning:

this is the end of land.
This is the end,
the last of all places I could be:

a stretch of beach, a hammock,
a pen and a pad, a letter
no email could contain.

The Big Dipper pours
night into the Gulf,
waves spread it into a fog

of black water, thick
beyond the last rings of light
around my single pier,

the last arm of the earth reaching
out its empty hand to abyss.

Occam's Razor

The clock's hands drift together,
a pair of scissor's closing on a string.
He cannot think of a time
when Alice has ever been late.

She's had a flat tire,
and her cell phone died,
and no one will stop,
not the police nor anybody

Or someone stopped and

Or she had to work late
and the phones aren't working
and her cell phone has no reception
and none of her friends are in the building

And the hands swing finally past 10:50

Khipu

As Alice twists the cord around her finger,
she makes a small knot at the center point,
then twists again intently as if to say
that we should talk. And knots again
the string atop the first bundle. Silently,
she twists an end of twine over the other,
forming a loop that closes the snarl of string.
She speaks in starts and stops, a different knot
on her tongue, an expectation she can't explain.
Again and again she twists the ends, never
looking up and never stopping, building
layers of knots, clenching a tight bulb
of the initial tension of two ends of string,
now constrained in a clump that speaks instead.

The Falling Away From

Nothing falls like snow,
shifting from a milk of cloud
to the warm street – Nothing,
not a feather, not ash, not
dust motes, not the stars
that are thrown from our Milky Way
into the expanse that surrounds deep space.

On SDSSJ090745–8, the eighth planet
from a star that we call Rogue,
Alice and I tell stories from fallen
generations of brighter nights.
We gorge our children with myths
of the stampede from the sky
of ram and fish and bull and lion;
little eyes tremble with tales of stellar
heroes abandoning their posts slowly.

Our sky empties as we fall away.
The rosy stars pale to become
distant carnations, familiar pinpricks
becoming dust motes, and finally,
like snow fallen on asphalt,
they disappear.

Event Horizon

The clock's hands are running laps
toward his departure time;
there is no good language
for goodbyes, no such thing
as simple goodbyes. So

Bob selects a line of string,
two ends taut with their separation;
this he folds into figure eights,
a series of them overlapping, combining,
the two tips set snugly together. Dew

settles on the grass; a cab bleats
behind the front door. He holds this spiral
above the envelope with her name on it,
and rethinks, and cuts the loops cleanly through.

Scale of apparent magnitudes

-26.73 Sun
-12.6   Full Moon
-10.3   A red ball
-9.5   Maximum brightness of an Iridium Flare
-7.8   A closing door
-4.7   Maximum brightness of Venus
-4.3   A length of string
-3.9   Faintest objects seen during the day with naked eye
-2.9   Maximum brightness of Mars
-1.5   Brightest star: Sirius
-0.7   Second brightest star: Canopus
0   The zero point by definition: This used to be Vega
2.9   A single blonde hair on a blue pillow
3   Faintest stars visible in an urban neighborhood